SELF-MANAGEMENT:
Promoting Success
in the
Middle-School Student

by
DAVID W. WILSON, Ph.D. & RUTH ANN WILSON

SCHOOL OF EDUCATION
CURRICULUM LABORATORY
UM-DEARBORN

COPYRIGHT © 1996 Mark Twain Media, Inc.

ISBN 1-58037-041-1

Printing No. CD-1896

Mark Twain Media, Inc., Publishers
Distributed by Carson-Dellosa Publishing Company, Inc.

Table of Contents

Introduction

This book is a practical tool for middle-school teachers interested in helping their students gain self-control over problem behaviors that can interfere with academic success. The issues addressed include motivation to learn, goal-setting, managing time, controlling anger and aggression, managing stress, and working effectively with others.

Principles inherent in effective **self-management** are utilized throughout the book. An emphasis is placed on the following concepts:

* *self-awareness*, e.g.,
    - recognition of one's feelings, beliefs, and behaviors, including how these compare to society's norms and values and how they compare to one's intended outcomes
    - recognition of one's attributes and skills
    - recognition of one's deficits and their causes
* *evaluation of alternative behaviors/recognizing and setting a value on the consequences of those behaviors*
* *setting goals*
* *developing plans/making decisions*
* *self-reinforcement*

Each unit of this book focuses on one particular problem area and consists of two basic sections:

(1) **Teacher Resource Pages.** The first section of the teacher resource material contains practical suggestions for promoting self-management and for controlling and correcting the problem being addressed. The recommendations are derived from what is known about that subject in the professional and scientific literature. The next part of the teacher resource material provides examples of activities that can be carried out with individual students or the entire class. Finally, a bibliography is provided for teachers who may want to consult some of the relevant literature.

(2) **Student Reproducible Pages.** In these pages, students are asked to reflect upon and write about the particular problem behavior. The purpose is to involve students actively and personally in recognizing and confronting the problem. By doing such things as answering questions, making choices, analyzing their behavior and its consequences, setting goals, and developing plans, students are nudged toward an acceptance of personal responsibility for their behavior and life outcomes. It is important for teachers to take an active role in working with students on these pages—helping clarify responses, providing feedback, and, in the process, gaining valuable diagnostic information.

—THE AUTHORS—

MOTIVATING STUDENTS TO LEARN

Tips for the Teacher

Motivating students is one of the most important tasks facing a teacher. Students who are motivated to learn strive for success and high standards of excellence. They have positive attitudes toward hard work and enjoy mastering difficult, challenging tasks.

Suggestions for Motivating Students:

Classroom environment. Students' efforts must be supported and encouraged, and students must feel comfortable taking risks. Lessening students' anxieties about learning is a good way to increase their motivation.

Modeling. Model behaviors and attitudes that are conducive to student motivation. Students will be more motivated to learn when they see teachers display enthusiasm, intensity, and a desire to learn.

Expectations. Communicate to students the expectation that they will be attentive, curious, task-oriented, motivated, capable of learning, and capable of a high level of performance. Students tend to behave in ways expected of them.

Intrinsic motivation. Find ways to arouse students' interest in what is being learned:

* Whenever possible, use activities, materials, and examples that students will relate to and enjoy.

* Maintain students' interest by varying the presentational format.

* Provide clear expectations and objectives for assigned material and tasks.

* Get students actively involved in the material through such means as games and experiments.

* Have assigned activities in which students interact with each other in structured and worthwhile ways that are related to lesson objectives.

* Give students immediate and steady feedback on their efforts and progress. Consistent opportunities to self-correct and make adjustments are important in maintaining students' interest in the task at hand.

Extrinsic motivation. Link students' learning with valued outcomes:

* Reward students' efforts, progress, and accomplishments by administering praise and other consequences valued by the students. Make it clear why the rewards are being given and make the rewards contingent on desirable behavior.

* Explain and demonstrate to students how their acquired knowledge and skills will be useful in gaining access to desired outcomes in everyday life (e.g., a particular career).

Attributional style. Students are most highly motivated when they attribute their *failures* not to a lack of ability, but rather, to a lack of effort, a lack of the appropriate information needed for success, or the use of inappropriate strategies for learning. They are most highly motivated when they attribute their *successes* to both ability and effort. In either case, teachers should nurture and reinforce these particular attributions.

Setting goals. Help students set goals for themselves. Enlist their commitment to the goals. Assist students in an evaluation of their progress toward those goals. Guide them toward a comparison of their current knowledge and skills to their previous levels of accomplishment or to some appropriate and desired standard. Remind students to self-reinforce when they make gains resulting from their efforts. (See GOAL-SETTING, page 13.)

Ensuring success. Students must experience some degree of success, and consistently so, if they are to be motivated. In other words, they must expect that, given the necessary effort, they will be successful. This suggests that teachers must present material at a level of difficulty appropriate to the children at a given point in time.

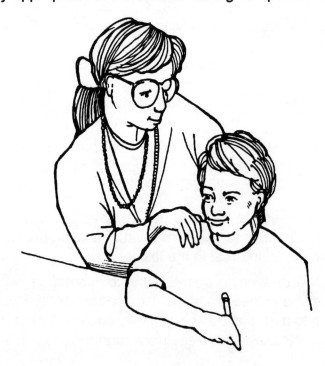

Suggestions for Individual or Group Activities:

* Let students make some choices about how they practice mastering a new skill. Such choices could include things like reviewing with a partner, working independently on a worksheet, or playing a game. Being able to make choices that work best for them will foster self-reliance in the students and help maintain their interest.

* Encourage students to help each other learn. They can do this by working together, serving as peer tutors, teaching shortcuts they have discovered, and giving verbal support.

* Record students' progress by preparing a chart with their names down the left side and a list of assignments across the top. As students finish assignments, they mark the appropriate columns by their names. Include extra credit activities for students who finish early. Grades could be based on earning points designated for each assignment listed on the chart.

* Provide students with a fun activity that allows them to use new skills. For example, after learning to divide fractions, students could divide the amounts of ingredients in a recipe to make individual servings. Students could then make individual servings using the new recipe amounts.

* Post pictures of students working in the classroom. Put articles and pictures in school newsletters and local newspapers about things students are learning.

* Intermittently reinforce desired classroom behaviors, such as working quietly or making positive statements, by handing out "chance tickets" to those students "caught being good." Hold a weekly drawing of chance tickets for prizes such as pencils, coupons for class privileges, or free items from book clubs.

* Ask students to interview adults in the community regarding their careers. Students could ask about such things as education and skills needed, job activities, and enjoyable aspects of the work. Have students report their findings to the rest of the class.

* Help students overcome negative thoughts and self-perceptions that they have when failing or doing poorly. To instill more positive, optimistic thinking, have students do the following:

    – *Become more aware of their negative thinking.* Point out to students the negative thoughts they verbalize. Have them write down those thoughts.

    – *Develop the skill of arguing against and counteracting negative thoughts.* To facilitate this, students need to recall instances of past success that make it more difficult to cling to negative self-perceptions such as "I am too dumb to get this." Have students write down their negative thoughts in one column and for each such thought, have them write a counter-thought that is more positive in a second column. For example, if the student's negative thought is "I'm too stupid; there's no reason to even try," the counter-thought might be "I did get a good grade in that subject last week; there is no reason why I can't do that again if I work hard."

* Have students keep daily classroom journals about what happened at school. Before students leave each day, ask them to think and write about things they learned, effective ways they studied, and things that hindered or improved their learning.

* Teach test-taking skills to help students feel like they "can do it." Give students sample tests and point out such strategies as skipping questions they do not know and working on them last, rereading questions after they have answered them to make sure the answers make sense, identifying key words in the questions, and eliminating obviously wrong answers in multiple-choice questions.

Bibliography

Brophy, J. (1987). Synthesis of research on strategies for motivating students to learn. *Educational Leadership, 45,* 40–48.

Dweck, C. S. (1975). The role of expectations and attributions in the alleviation of learned helplessness. *Journal of Personality and Social Psychology, 31,* 674–685.

Mayer, F. S., & Sutton, K. (1996). *Personality: An integrative approach.* Upper Saddle River, NJ: Prentice Hall.

Mischel, W. (1993). *Introduction to personality* (5th ed.). Fort Worth, TX: Harcourt Brace Jovanovich.

Seligman, M. E. P. (1990). *Learned optimism.* New York: Knopf.

Slavin, R. E. (1994). *Educational psychology: Theory and practice* (4th ed.). Needham Heights, MA: Allyn & Bacon.

Van Houten, R. (1980). *How to motivate others through feedback.* Austin, TX: PRO–ED.

Name _____ Date _____

Measuring Your Motivation to Learn

In order to be more motivated, it is useful to first recognize your current level of motivation. Answering the following items may help you figure out how motivated you really are.

Circle the number and word or phrase that make each statement true for you.

1. I enjoy school.

0	1	2	3
never	rarely	often	very often

2. I enjoy hard work.

0	1	2	3
never	rarely	often	very often

3. I like difficult, challenging assignments.

0	1	2	3
never	rarely	often	very often

4. I enjoy trying to do better than others in my class.

0	1	2	3
never	rarely	often	very often

5. I enjoy trying to improve at something.

0	1	2	3
never	rarely	often	very often

6. I like to learn about new things even when I don't have to.

0	1	2	3
never	rarely	often	very often

7. When I am given something new to learn, I expect to be successful.

0	1	2	3
never	rarely	often	very often

Name _____ Date _____

8. I enjoy learning.

0	1	2	3
never	rarely	often	very often

9. When I get up in the morning, I can't wait to get to school.

0	1	2	3
never	rarely	often	very often

10. I believe that going to school will help me be successful in life.

0	1	2	3
never	rarely	often	very often

Add up the numbers you circled. The total is your **Motivation to Learn Score.**

My score is: _____

0–10 points: You do not appear to be very motivated at the present time. Learning does not seem to be much fun for you. Talk to your teacher about ways you might become more motivated.

11–20 points: You seem to be motivated some of the time. Learning is somewhat and sometimes fun for you. Talk to your teacher about things you might do to stay motivated.

21–30 points: You appear to be very motivated to learn. Learning seems to be fun for you. You are excited about learning and look forward to school.

Do you agree with your **Motivation to Learn Score**? _____ Why? _____

_____

_____

Would your teachers agree with you about your score? _____ Why? _____

_____

_____

Would your parents agree with you about your score? _____ Why? _____

_____

_____

Name _____ Date _____

Thinking About Success and Failure

Your desire to learn may very well depend on how you explain your successes and failures. Think about a time in the past when you did well on some test or assignment. Why did you do well? For each of the following possible explanations, circle "Yes" or "No."

"I did well because . . ."

it was easy.	Yes	No
I was lucky.	Yes	No
the teacher was an easy grader.	Yes	No
I tried hard.	Yes	No
I am smart.	Yes	No
I knew how to study.	Yes	No
I knew exactly what the teacher wanted me to do.	Yes	No

Can you give other reasons? _____

_____

Explain your answers. _____

_____

Think about a time in the past when you did not do well on some test or assignment. Why didn't you do well? For each of the following possible explanations, circle "Yes" or "No."

"I did poorly because . . ."

it was too hard.	Yes	No
I had bad luck.	Yes	No
the teacher was a hard grader.	Yes	No
I didn't really try.	Yes	No
I am dumb.	Yes	No
I didn't know how to study.	Yes	No
I didn't understand the instructions.	Yes	No

Can you give other reasons? _____

_____

Explain your answers. _____

_____

Name _____ Date _____

Before an Exam

Before an exam, do you expect to do well? (check one)

_____ Always
_____ Most of the time
_____ Sometimes
_____ Rarely
_____ Never

Why? _____

Before an exam, does your teacher expect you to do well?

_____ Always
_____ Most of the time
_____ Sometimes
_____ Rarely
_____ Never

Why? _____

Thinking Good Thoughts

It is easier to be motivated when you think good things about yourself. Often, though, when students do poorly, they think bad things about themselves. In the column on the left below, there are some examples of such bad thoughts. In the right column, practice thinking good things about yourself by writing an alternative good thought across from each bad thought. An example of a good thought is provided.

Bad Thoughts	Alternative Good Thoughts
I'm stupid.	*I'm not stupid. I just need to work harder to do better.*
I can't do anything.	_____
I am the dumbest kid in class.	_____
I can't remember anything.	_____
I am terrible at math.	_____
I always do poorly on tests.	_____
No one likes me.	_____
I give up.	_____

Name _____ Date _____

Your Interests and Strengths

In School

Even if you are having difficulty getting interested in school, there are probably some things about school that you like and some things that you are good at doing. What are those things?

What do you like the most about school?

1. _____

2. _____

3. _____

What are you good at doing in school?

1. _____

2. _____

3. _____

Out of School

Now think about things you like and things you are good at doing when you are not in school.

When you are not in school, what do you like doing?

1. _____

2. _____

3. _____

What are you good at doing when you are not in school?

1. _____

2. _____

3. _____

Name _____ Date _____

Thinking About How to be More Successful

Think of some things you could do that would help you be more successful in the classroom. Check each of these possibilities that you think would be helpful.

_____ 1. Sit in a different place in class.

_____ 2. Study with friends.

_____ 3. Get more help from the teacher.

_____ 4. Keep up with assignments.

_____ 5. Come to school well-rested.

_____ 6. Listen better in class.

_____ 7. Find ways to get interested in the material being studied.

_____ 8. Work on improving study and test-taking skills.

_____ 9. Work on using my time more wisely.

_____ 10. Ask my parents or brothers and sisters for help.

Is there another step you think would be helpful?

_____ 11. _____

Consider each item that you checked. List those items below in order from most helpful to least helpful.

1. _____

2. _____

3. _____

4. _____

5. _____

6. _____

7. _____

8. _____

9. _____

10. _____

11. _____

Name _____ Date _____

Good Things from Learning

It is easier to be motivated to learn if you value learning, think it is important, and believe that good things will happen to you as a result of your learning. List as many good things as you can that might happen if you work hard in school and learn as much as you can.

1. *I will make good grades.*

2. *I will feel* _____

3. _____

4. _____

5. _____

6. _____

7. _____

8. _____

9. _____

10. _____

Do you think that studying mathematics, science, language, social studies, and other subjects will help you in your life? (check one)

    Yes _____

    No _____

Explain your answer.

_____

_____

_____

_____

_____

Name _____ Date _____

Your Plans for the Future

It is easier to be motivated to learn if you have some plans for the future that involve using what you are learning. Think for a moment about some of your plans.

Do you plan on graduating from high school? (check one)

        Yes _____
        No _____

Why? _____

_____

Do you plan on going to college?

        Yes _____
        No _____

Why? _____

_____

Do you plan on having a job when you get out of school?

        Yes _____
        No _____

If yes, what type of job do you hope to have?

_____

What are you learning in school now that will be needed for the job?

_____

_____

How much education and what types of skills do you need for the job?

_____

_____

If you are not planning on having a job, what do you plan on doing?

_____

_____

GOAL-SETTING

Tips for the Teacher

A **goal** is any outcome a person intends to achieve at some future date. Successful people set goals, develop plans, and then work toward achieving their goals. For those who want to improve themselves or change their behavior, goal-setting is a critical activity.

Suggestions for Helping Students Set Goals:

Identifying goals. Students should identify their goals and write them down. This writing process forces students to clarify their goals and to focus on them.

* *Goals should be as specific as possible.* For one thing, specific goals are more motivating than general, vague goals. Secondly, specific goals are more well-defined and, thus, more easily measured. Goals must be observable and measurable if students are to know if improvement is occurring.

* *Large goals may need to be broken down into smaller goals.* Large goals can sometimes be overwhelming and discouraging. Breaking such goals into smaller, more manageable parts allows students to establish momentum and confidence.

* *Goals should be realistic yet challenging.* Goals that are too easy or too hard are not as motivating as goals that are moderately difficult but realistically attainable.

Developing plans. Students need to develop plans for achieving their goals. Steps toward goal achievement should be outlined, prioritized, and recorded. In developing plans, students need to consider factors in their favor as well as potential problems. Plans should also include target dates for completing the goals.

Monitoring progress. Students should record progress toward their goals by observing their behavior and constructing tables, charts, or graphs. If they are dissatisfied with their progress, they should make appropriate adjustments in their plans or they should re-evaluate their goals. Feedback from such monitoring provides opportunities for students to reward themselves for making progress toward their goals and alerts teachers to opportunities to reward the students as well.

Committing to goals. The teacher can be a positive influence on students' commitment or motivation by supporting and rewarding students' goal-directed behavior. Commitment is enhanced as well when students set their own goals, when they reward themselves for goal-directed behavior, when they expect to achieve their goals, and when they have experienced prior success in attaining difficult goals. Supportive peers also strengthen goal commitment.

Suggestions for Individual or Group Activities:

* Have all students set personal and academic goals for themselves at the beginning of the semester. At the end of the semester, students should evaluate their progress toward those goals and set goals for the future (see page 18 for an example of a goal-setting sheet).

* Help students on an individual basis set goals for specific behaviors that need to be changed. For example, a student who speaks out inappropriately during class may set as a goal: "I will raise my hand and be recognized before speaking in class." Such individual goals should be monitored frequently by the student and the teacher together. This gives the teacher opportunities for verbal and other types of reinforcement.

* Encourage students to record their daily assignments (see page 19 for a sample assignment sheet). Students should mark off assignments as they are completed. At the end of the day, students can easily check for any unfinished work to be taken home for completion.

* Post "Goal-Setting Tips" in the classroom (see page 20 for such a list).

* Help students believe they can achieve their goals by:

    – conveying confidence in their ability to achieve their goals.
    – alerting students to models who have successfully achieved similar goals.
    – helping students associate pleasant feelings with achieving their goals.
    – recognizing and rewarding progress toward achieving their goals.

* In order to facilitate goal commitment, have students share their goals with another student and prompt them to help each other toward goal achievement. This support system should be useful at all stages—when students are identifying their goals, developing plans for goal achievement, and monitoring goal progress.

Bibliography

Bandura, A. (1977). Self-efficacy: Toward a unifying theory of behavioral change. *Psychological Review, 84,* 191–215.

Hollenbeck, J. R., & Klein, H. J. (1987). Goal commitment and the goal-setting process: Problems, prospects, and proposals for future research. *Journal of Applied Psychology, 72,* 212–220.

Locke, E. A., & Latham, G. P. (1990). *A theory of goal setting and task performance.* Englewood Cliffs, NJ: Prentice-Hall.

Maddux, J. E. (1991). Personal efficacy. In V. J. Derlega, B. A. Winstead, & W. H. Jones (Eds.), *Personality: Contemporary theory and research* (pp. 231–261). Chicago: Nelson-Hall.

Name _____ Date _____

Setting Goals and Making Plans

A **goal** is anything you hope to achieve in the future. If you want to improve yourself or change your behavior, it is very important to set goals and then work toward achieving them.

Current Goals

What are three of your current academic goals?

1._____

2._____

3._____

What are three of your current personal goals?

1._____

2._____

3._____

A Plan of Action

From the list above, pick the goal that is most important to you.

The goal: _____

How difficult will it be to achieve this goal? (pick one)

_____ Very difficult
_____ Moderately difficult
_____ Somewhat difficult
_____ Not at all difficult

What problems might you have trying to reach this goal?

_____

_____

_____

Name _____ Date _____

What help might you need to be able to reach this goal? From whom can you get this help?

_____

_____

_____

What new knowledge or skills do you need to be able to reach this goal?

_____

_____

_____

What is your plan for achieving your goal? In other words, what specific steps do you plan on taking to reach the goal? List those steps in the order in which they need to be done.

1._____

2._____

3._____

4._____

5._____

When do you hope to reach this goal?_____

How could you keep track of your progress toward achieving this goal?

_____

_____

_____

When you make good progress toward your goal or eventually achieve your goal, what type of reward could you give yourself (or what type of reward could your teacher give you)?

_____

_____

Name _____ Date _____

How sure are you that you will be able to achieve this particular goal? (pick one)

_____ Not at all sure
_____ Somewhat sure
_____ Moderately sure
_____ Very sure

If you are "not at all sure" or "somewhat sure," why is that so?

_____

_____

_____

_____

How important to you is this goal? Why?

_____

_____

_____

_____

What good things might happen to you when you attain this goal?

_____

_____

_____

_____

_____

_____

_____

Name _____ Date _____

SEMESTER GOALS

Set goals for yourself at the beginning of the semester. At the end of the semester, give yourself 5 points if the goal has been achieved, 3 points if you have made some progress toward the goal, and 1 point if you have not made much progress toward the goal.

Personal Goals

List three things you plan to work toward personally this semester. For example, "I want to save enough money to buy a CD player."

1. _____   5   3   1

2. _____   5   3   1

3. _____   5   3   1

Academic Goals

List three things you plan to work toward academically this semester. For example, "I want to improve my spelling grade."

1. _____   5   3   1

2. _____   5   3   1

3. _____   5   3   1

SUPER
Goal-Setter

Name _____ Date _____

Assignment Sheet

Write down each assignment. Fill in the bubble when the assignment is finished. Before leaving school for the day, check the bubbles to see what work needs to be completed at home.

LANGUAGE

O Mon. _____

O Tues. _____

O Wed. _____

O Thurs. _____

O Fri. _____

SPELLING

O Mon. _____

O Tues. _____

O Wed. _____

O Thurs. _____

O Fri. _____

READING

O Mon. _____

O Tues. _____

O Wed. _____

O Thurs. _____

O Fri. _____

SOCIAL STUDIES

O Mon. _____

O Tues. _____

O Wed. _____

O Thurs. _____

O Fri. _____

MATHEMATICS

O Mon. _____

O Tues. _____

O Wed. _____

O Thurs. _____

O Fri. _____

SCIENCE

O Mon. _____

O Tues. _____

O Wed. _____

O Thurs. _____

O Fri. _____

GOAL-SETTING TIPS

1. Set a goal and write it down.

2. Make your goal hard but possible.

3. Set a target date.

4. Make a plan and write it down.

5. Keep track of your progress.

6. Reward yourself for success.

7. Be patient. Reaching a difficult goal takes time and hard work.

TIME MANAGEMENT

Tips for the Teacher

Many students fail to achieve their full potential because they do not manage their time well. An important task for teachers is to help students identify their particular time management problems and then assist them in overcoming those problems.

Suggestions for Helping Students Manage Their Time:

Goals and priorities. It is difficult to convince students that managing time is important unless they are goal-oriented. If students have goals and priorities, motivation and careful planning take precedence over bewilderment, floundering, and wasting time. Encourage students to set goals and to prioritize them. (See GOAL-SETTING, page 13.)

Perfectionism. Striving for perfection can be ultimately self-defeating because perfection is too elusive an ideal. Seeking perfection on a task often results in never completing that task or losing valuable time that could be spent on other tasks. Work with students to temper their perfectionistic tendencies and to focus on doing the best they can.

Procrastination. There are many reasons for procrastination. Some students have unrealistic expectations about achievement. They want to do a task perfectly but then procrastinate when they realize that perfection is unlikely. Others simply are fearful and are overwhelmed by a task. They do not know where to begin and so do not start. Still others daydream or are easily distracted by trivial aspects of their work. Simple prompting may help get these particular students started. Whatever the origin of the problem, there are some basic steps that should be helpful for any procrastinating student:

* Identify and prioritize the tasks that need to be completed.
* Have realistic goals for each task.
* Plan for each task by identifying a series of small steps that need to be carried out to complete the task.
* Work out a time schedule for completing each of those small steps.
* Execute the plan, beginning with the most important task.
* If procrastination continues to be a problem, identify even smaller steps that could be taken in order to complete a given task.
* Continuously monitor and record progress on each task.
* Reward yourself for completing each step of the plan.

Overload. Children, like adults, can take on too many responsibilities and activities—more than they can comfortably handle without feeling physically fatigued and mentally overwhelmed. Discuss the matter with children and their parents when overload is identified as a potential problem.

Impatience. Some students are impatient. They tend to hurry through assignments and focus more on "getting it done" than on the quality of their work. Productivity suffers and time is wasted when poor work has to be redone. Urge impatient students to slow down, think about what they are doing, and focus on quality. Reinforce the quality of their work as much as the speed of its completion.

Feedback and reinforcement. Provide students with feedback and reinforcement for appropriate time management behaviors. For example, reinforce such things as keeping desks uncluttered and turning in assignments on time. Also, remind students to self-reward their efforts at better time management.

Optimal conditions. Time management tends to be less of a problem when students are relatively free of physical, mental, and environmental problems. If students come to school fatigued, sick, or plagued with personal problems, they inevitably will have difficulties concentrating and getting their work done in a timely fashion. Similar outcomes can be expected when students do not have optimal study environments free of interruptions and distractions. Teachers should be attentive to these sorts of problems and work with the students, parents, and other staff to get the problems corrected as soon as possible.

Organization. For some students, time management is made more difficult by their lack of organizational skills and habits. These students need practical advice from teachers on how to get better organized. For example, students may need help with such things as setting goals, prioritizing tasks, developing a filing system for keeping track of things to be done, and scheduling study time.

Time budget. A good way to avoid wasting time is to budget time by making a schedule. Students obviously have a number of "free hours" before and after school and in the evenings that they can budget. Assist students in working out weekly schedules for these hours so that blocks of time are scheduled for eating, recreation, family responsibilities, and studying. Such budgeting will help ensure that important school-related tasks get done in a timely fashion. Discuss with students the advantages and disadvantages of doing certain tasks at specific times (e.g., the advantages of doing school work when one is well-rested or when there is the best opportunity for quiet time).

Suggestions for Individual or Group Activities:

* Help students work toward a resolution of their time management problems. Have them:
     (1) identify their problems.
     (2) recognize which problems are the biggest.
     (3) analyze causes of their problems.
     (4) identify possible solutions and select the best solutions.
     (5) set goals for overcoming the problems.
     (6) make plans for achieving those goals.

Begin the above analysis by having the entire class work together in a brainstorming exercise. After some group discussion related to the identification of problems, their causes, and their possible solutions, have students work alone in establishing personal goals and plans. Following such individual work, have students share their plans with each other. Encourage students to support each other.

* Prompt students to get organized by posting relevant tips and strategies. (See "Tips for Getting Organized" on page 32.)

* Have surprise desk or locker inspections to look for clean, neat, and organized conditions. Give a small reward to those who "pass inspection."

* Motivate students to keep organized by helping them develop a filing system (e.g., use portfolios) for assignments they are working on, completed assignments, and returned work.

* Find age-appropriate mazes and have students try to draw a line through each maze while looking at it in a mirror. Challenge students to draw the line without touching any part of the maze boundaries. Doing this task without making any mistakes requires that students be patient, slow, and careful as they work. It should be a good patience-building assignment for impatient, hurry-prone students. Emphasize to students your desire for high-quality work. Motivate them to slow down and focus on doing the task well. If students find the task too easy, have them use their non-dominant hands. (See page 33 for a sample maze.)

Bibliography

Ellis, D. B. (1991). *Becoming a master student* (6th ed.). Rapid City, SD: College Survival, Inc.

Greenberg, J. S. (1996). *Comprehensive stress management* (5th ed.). Madison, WI: Brown and Benchmark.

Morgan, C. T., & Deese, J. (1969). *How to study* (2nd ed.). New York: McGraw-Hill.

Rice, P. L. (1987). *Stress and health: Principles and practice for coping and wellness.* Monterey, CA: Brooks/Cole.

Schafer, W. (1987). *Stress management for wellness.* New York: Holt, Rinehart and Winston.

Sternberg, R. J. (1988). *The triarchic mind: A new theory of human intelligence.* New York: Penguin.

Name _____ Date _____

Measuring Your Time Management Skills

In order to do a better job of managing your time in the future, it is useful to first recognize how good or poor a job you are doing right now. Answering the following items may help you figure out how big a problem time management is for you.

Circle the number and word or phrase that make each statement true for you.

1. I turn in my assignments late.

0	1	2	3
never	rarely	often	very often

2. I waste time.

0	1	2	3
never	rarely	often	very often

3. I have trouble getting everything done that I am supposed to do.

0	1	2	3
never	rarely	often	very often

4. Noises and people around me bother me when I'm working.

0	1	2	3
never	rarely	often	very often

5. I try to do things perfectly.

0	1	2	3
never	rarely	often	very often

6. I have trouble finding things when I need them.

0	1	2	3
never	rarely	often	very often

7. I wait too long to begin working on an assignment.

0	1	2	3
never	rarely	often	very often

Name _____ Date _____

8. When I go somewhere, I show up late.

0	1	2	3
never	rarely	often	very often

9. I like to get my work done in a hurry.

0	1	2	3
never	rarely	often	very often

10. I feel rushed.

0	1	2	3
never	rarely	often	very often

Add up the numbers you circled. The total is your **Time Management Score.**

My score is _____ .

    0–10 points: You appear to be doing a good job of managing your time.
    11–20 points: You appear to have time management problems some of the time. Talk to your teacher and get help before the problems get any worse.
    21–30 points: You appear to have time management problems much or most of the time. These problems are bad enough to affect your school work.

Do you agree with your **Time Management Score**? _____ Why? _____

_____

_____

Would your teachers agree with you about your score? _____ Why? _____

_____

_____

Would your parents agree with you about your score? _____ Why? _____

_____

_____

_____

Name _____ Date _____

Consequences of Managing Time Well or Poorly

It is useful to think about the consequences of managing your time well or poorly. Hopefully, you can see that there are many good things about having good time management skills and many bad things about having poor time management skills.

What might happen if you do a poor job of managing your time?

1._____

2._____

3._____

4._____

5._____

What might happen if you do a good job of managing your time?

1._____

2._____

3._____

4._____

5._____

What conclusions can you draw from studying the above lists?

_____

_____

_____

_____

_____

_____

Name _____ Date _____

Your Biggest Time Management Problems

What are the biggest problems you have right now with managing your time (e.g., putting things off that you need to do)?

1. _____

2. _____

3. _____

4. _____

5. _____

6. _____

7. _____

Time Management Goals

List some things about managing your time that you would like to improve. Be specific. For example, you might say, "I would like to turn in my assignments on time."

1. _____

2. _____

3. _____

4. _____

5. _____

6. _____

7. _____

Name _____ Date _____

A Plan for Success

Develop a plan for improving the way you manage your time. What specific steps could you take? List them below. An example is written already.

1. *Ask the teacher for help.* _____

2. _____

3. _____

4. _____

5. _____

6. _____

7. _____

8. _____

9. _____

10. _____

Self-Rewards

List things you enjoy that could be used to reward yourself when you make progress toward managing your time better.

1. _____

2. _____

3. _____

4. _____

5. _____

Name _____ Date _____

Putting Tasks in a Logical Order

It is easy to waste time when you do not know what to do, what to do first, or what to do next. Any big assignment should first be broken down into small steps, and then those steps should be carried out in a logical order. Below are small steps for writing a book report. Study the steps carefully. Then put the steps in an order that makes sense. Remember: some steps need to be carried out before other steps.

Steps for writing a book report:

1. Read the book.
2. Write a rough draft of the report.
3. Go to the library.
4. Make an outline of the report.
5. Write the final draft of the report.
6. Check out a book.
7. Have someone else read the report and give feedback.

Now put those steps in the order in which you believe they should be done:

1._____

2._____

3._____

4._____

5._____

6._____

7._____

Now have your teacher check your ordering.

SCHOOL OF EDUCATION
CURRICULUM LABORATORY
UM-DEARBORN

MAKING A SCHEDULE

Make a schedule for how you will spend your free time before school, after school, and in the evenings. Here are some tips to keep in mind as you make your schedule:

1. Find a balance in your schedule. Include time for:
   * eating
   * recreation (fun)
   * chores and other family responsibilities
   * school work

2. Set your bedtime first and build the rest of the schedule around that.

3. In scheduling time for homework and studying, find times that work best for you—times when you will be the most well-rested and efficient.

4. Don't short-change study time. Studying is important. Remember that you need to avoid putting things off and you need to avoid doing things at the last minute.

5. Don't forget to schedule some short breaks during your study periods.

6. In the study periods of your schedule, list exactly what you will be working on whenever possible. If you have a book report due, you might write "read book for book report."

7. Make a new schedule each week so you can update and change what needs to be done.

8. Be realistic. Allow enough time for each item in your schedule.

9. Allow for some flexibility in your schedule. Be prepared for the unexpected.

10. Ask the teacher for feedback on your schedule after you complete it.

Name _____ Date _____

My Schedule

Week of _____

Time	Monday	Tuesday	Wednesday	Thursday	Friday
A.M.					
5:00					
6:00					
7:00					
8:00					
P.M.					
3:00					
4:00					
5:00					
6:00					
7:00					
8:00					
9:00					
10:00					
11:00					
12:00					

TIPS FOR GETTING ORGANIZED

1. Set goals and make plans. Know what needs to be done.

2. Figure out what's most important and do those tasks first.

3. Don't put off doing important tasks.

4. Avoid wasting time. Make a schedule.

5. Keep a daily "to do" list. Check off tasks as they are completed.

6. Keep your desk and locker neat and organized.

7. Have a system for keeping track of important papers and other materials.

8. Write down important things that you need to remember.

9. Have a quiet time each day in which you plan that day's or the next day's activities.

10. When your work is finished, reward yourself by doing something you enjoy.

Name ——————————————— Date ———————————————

Maze

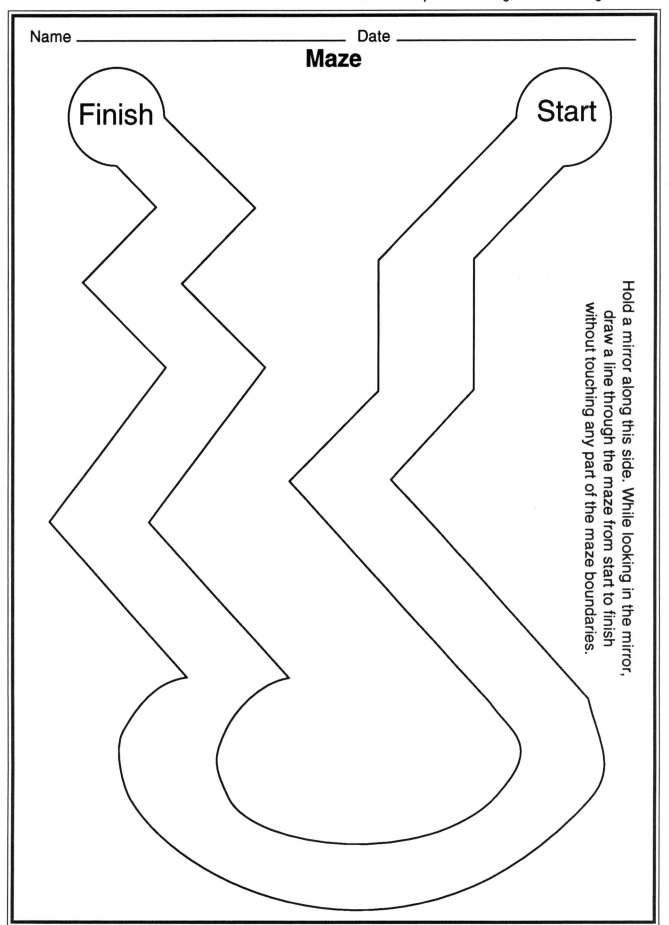

Hold a mirror along this side. While looking in the mirror, draw a line through the maze from start to finish without touching any part of the maze boundaries.

33

CONTROLLING ANGER AND AGGRESSION

Tips for the Teacher

Aggression is any behavior intended to inflict physical or psychological harm. It may be either physical or verbal in form. Anger is the emotion most commonly associated with aggression. Controlling anger and aggression is an important matter for teachers and students alike.

Suggestions for Controlling Aggression in the Classroom:

Make expectations and consequences clear. It is absolutely critical that students know what kind of behavior is expected of them and what the consequences will be when they violate those standards.

Follow through with consequences promptly and consistently. When aggression occurs, students should incur the consequences that were anticipated for such behavior. The consequences should be administered promptly following the aggressive act and should be carried out consistently whenever aggression occurs. Make sure that a consequence intended to be punishing is indeed so. For example, being forced to miss recess may actually be reinforcing rather than punishing for some students.

Model nonaggressive behavior. Children learn from models how to behave, what type of behavior is appropriate, and the consequences of a particular behavior. Therefore, avoid modeling aggressive behavior or thinking. Be a model of cooperative, prosocial behavior. Children need to see models who, when provoked, restrain themselves and engage in nonaggressive actions. Promptly extinguish any displays of aggression by the students to minimize their adverse modeling impact on others and to show that aggression is not tolerated.

Avoid reinforcing aggression. Given that aggression is maintained, in part, through reinforcement, try to remove the reinforcement. The teacher's attention and the interruption of class may serve as reinforcements for some children's aggression. Deal with such situations quickly and with as little fanfare and comment as possible. Prolonged attention from the teacher will serve only to encourage the aggression.

Reinforce prosocial behavior. While trying to extinguish aggression by not reinforcing it, also try to reinforce more positive, prosocial behavior when it occurs. In effect, "catch" children being good.

Utilize apologies. Once aggression has occurred, a sincere apology by the attacker that involves an explanation of the behavior and an acceptance of personal responsibility is useful in preventing any counterattacks. Since the apology needs to be thoughtful and sincere, do not demand an immediate apology from the student.

Teach problem-solving and communication skills. Teach children to focus on their problems as situations demanding solutions, of which there are many alternatives. Emphasize that each of those alternatives needs to be evaluated in terms of its consequences as well as its effectiveness in solving the problem. When discussing aggression, teach children that when they have problems that make them angry, they should search for solutions that are both effective (i.e., their anger and the conflict are reduced) and nonhurtful. Many children need help in learning how to handle their anger arising from such sources as criticism, teasing, and physical provocation. Assist them by emphasizing constructive solutions like negotiation, compromise, seeking assistance, talking to parents or another adult about their problems, and other forms of verbal communication.

More generally, students should be encouraged to engage in the following thought sequence when they experience anger:

1. *STOP! THINK!* **(achievement of cognitive control over the emotion)**
2. *What am I feeling? Is this anger?* **(self-awareness)**
3. *If I am angry, why am I angry? Is my anger justified? Do I have a sufficient cause to be angry? Is this something worth getting angry about or staying angry about? Is it possible I'd be better off trying not to be angry?* **(analysis of reasons for anger; justification/ nonjustification of anger)**

Examples of thoughts that would tend to lessen anger:
   * The attacker didn't really mean to hurt me.
   * Yes, I'm frustrated, but there's nothing unfair about it.
   * I'm not even sure why I'm angry.
   * The attacker apologized to me already.
   * The incident was pretty minor. I'm not hurt that badly.
   * The attacker has been having a lot of problems lately. I'm sure that's why he hurt me.
   * That's not like the attacker to hurt me. I don't think it will happen again.
   * The attacker is just trying to make me angry. I'm not going to let him win. It's not worth it to me to be angry all the time.
   * I started the dispute. I don't have a right to be angry.

Common responses given the above thoughts:
   * Tolerate the insult.
   * Laugh it off.
   * Forgive the attacker.
   * Forget about the incident—don't dwell on it.
   * Ignore the provocation.
   * Apologize for starting the conflict.
   * Accept the frustration/work constructively to overcome it.

4. *If I believe my anger is justified, how can I try to resolve the problem in a way that does not hurt anyone?* **(evaluation of various solution alternatives in terms of their consequences and effectiveness)**

Help children who consistently see hostile intent. Children who consistently see maliciousness and hostility in other people's actions need some attention. Such children need help in better understanding the varying intentions that can underlie a given behavior and help in discriminating between intentional and unintentional behavior. These children need to see the world in less threatening terms and to understand that sometimes a behavior that provoked them into anger and aggression was in fact accidental or had an intent other than provocation.

Encourage responses that cancel out anger. Sometimes aggression can be controlled by nurturing responses that tend to lessen anger because they are incompatible with it or because the angry person simply does not think about the anger. The following are effective strategies:

*   *Teach empathy.* Teach children empathy—the ability to understand and share someone else's feelings. Discuss with them how their actions affect other people. When someone is hurt, emphasize how that person feels. Having students role-play various situations like being teased, physically attacked, or unfairly criticized can help them better appreciate the victim's point of view. In short, feelings of concern for someone are incompatible with the anger and aggression that might otherwise be directed at that same person.

*   *Induce humor.* It is difficult as well to be angry and happy at the same time. There are times when the anger and tension in a situation can be alleviated through the injection of humor into the situation.

*   *Promote distraction from the source of anger.* Encourage students to turn away from angry thoughts and to avoid dwelling on what has made them angry. Help them find ways to distract themselves from what has angered them.

Watch for frustrations and provocations. Given the importance of frustration and provocation in instigating aggression, watch for these conditions during the school day and take appropriate actions to prevent their occurrence or to minimize their intensity or effects. For example, provocations on the playground when students are playing football at recess can easily carry over into the classroom later in the day. Awareness of such conflicts can help prevent any subsequent aggression (e.g., the teacher might make sure that two students involved in a dispute work apart from each other the rest of the day).

Reduce emotional arousal. Various sources of emotional arousal can facilitate aggressive behavior when people are angry. Students can experience arousal, for example, through running and jumping at recess or through the excitement associated with a class party. If, in the course of the day, a student gets angry, this arousal will increase the child's aggressive tendencies. The implication is this: be alert for high levels of arousal and work toward maintaining a calm classroom atmosphere.

Suggestions for Individual or Group Activities:

* Discuss with students at the beginning of the year expectations regarding aggressive behavior in the classroom. Students need to know that solving problems without hurting others is a skill valued by society and a skill that they will be able to develop through practice.

* Students may need assistance in understanding the definition of aggression and the various forms it can take. Put a list on the board of both aggressive and nonaggressive acts and have students discuss why each is or is not an example of aggression. As a result of such a discussion, students should better appreciate that aggression goes beyond just hitting others and better understand the role of intent to do harm in any act of aggression.

* Have the students make up a list of rules regarding "what to do when angry" and post the list in class. Critique the list with them, and discuss the importance of distinguishing between constructive and destructive ways of handling anger.

* When students have read something violent or watched a violent movie or television program, take advantage of the opportunity to discuss the violence. Discuss the reasons for the violence; the consequences of it; the reality of what was being depicted; the inappropriateness of violence and the inappropriateness of imitating it; and the fact that most people don't behave in this manner. Then aid the students in finding nonaggressive ways to solve their problems.

* As a general classroom principle, encourage students to give themselves a "cooling off" period when they are angry. Suggest, for example, that they count to 100 if angry. Or perhaps designate a special cooling off place students may go to as needed. Once the students have calmed down, talk to them and encourage them to deal constructively with any lingering anger.

Bibliography

Bandura, A. (1973). *Aggression: A social learning analysis.* Englewood Cliffs, NJ: Prentice-Hall.

Baron, R. A., & Richardson, D. R. (1994). *Human aggression* (2nd ed.). New York: Plenum.

Berkowitz, L. (1993). *Aggression: Its causes, consequences, and control.* New York: McGraw-Hill.

Geen, R. G. (1990). *Human aggression.* Pacific Grove, CA: Brooks/Cole.

Huesmann, L. R. (Ed.). (1994). *Aggressive behavior: Current perspectives.* New York: Plenum.

Wegner, D. M., & Pennbaker, J. W. (Eds.). (1993). *Handbook of mental control.* Englewood Cliffs, NJ: Prentice-Hall.

Williams, R., & Williams, V. (1993). *Anger kills: Seventeen strategies for controlling the hostility that can harm your health.* New York: Random House.

Wyer, R. S., Jr., & Srull, T. K. (Eds.). (1993). *Perspectives on anger and emotion.* Hillsdale, NJ: Erlbaum.

Name _____ Date _____

Measuring Your Anger Control

Think about the times you get angry. Answering the following items may help you figure out how much of a problem anger is in your life.

Circle the number and word or phrase that make each statement true for you.

1. My anger interferes with my school performance.

0	1	2	3
never	rarely	often	very often

2. My anger interferes with my making and keeping friends.

0	1	2	3
never	rarely	often	very often

3. My anger makes me worry about myself.

0	1	2	3
never	rarely	often	very often

4. My anger worries my parents.

0	1	2	3
never	rarely	often	very often

5. My anger gets me into trouble at home.

0	1	2	3
never	rarely	often	very often

6. My anger gets me into trouble at school.

0	1	2	3
never	rarely	often	very often

7. My anger has caused me to hurt people by calling them names or saying other mean things to them.

0	1	2	3
never	rarely	often	very often

Name _____ Date _____

8. My anger has caused me to hurt other people by hitting them or physically fighting with them.

      0   1   2   3

   never   rarely   often   very often

9. My anger has caused me to feel physically ill.

      0   1   2   3

   never   rarely   often   very often

10. My anger has caused me to destroy someone's property.

      0   1   2   3

   never   rarely   often   very often

Add up the numbers you circled. The total is your **Anger Control Score.**

My score is _____ .

     0–10 points: Anger does not seem to be much of a problem for you at the present time.

     11–20 points: Anger appears to be a mild problem in your life. Watch for any increase in the problem. Talk to your parents or teacher for advice.

     21–30 points: Anger appears to be affecting your life in many bad ways. Talk to your parents or teacher about things you can do to handle anger better.

Do you agree with your **Anger Control Score**? _____ Why? _____

_____

_____

Would your teachers agree with you about your score? _____ Why? _____

_____

_____

Would your parents agree with you about your score? _____ Why? _____

_____

_____

Name _____ Date _____

Analyzing Reasons for Others' Behaviors

Suppose you are playing kickball with other students. Someone kicks the ball and it hits you in the face, hurting you so badly that your nose bleeds.

List three possible reasons why the ball hit you in the face.

1. _____ . _____

2. _____

3. _____

Understanding How Others Feel
as a Result of Your Actions

Suppose you have just hurt someone by calling that person a mean name.

Describe how you think that person would feel as a result of your actions.

_____

_____

Why would the person feel this way?

_____

_____

If someone were to hurt you in the same way, how would you feel?

_____

_____

Why?

_____

_____

_____

Name _____ Date _____

A Problem Situation

When was the last time you were angry? _____

_____

Why were you angry? What was the problem? _____

_____

What caused the problem? Why did it happen? _____

_____

_____

Did you have a **real** reason to be angry? Why or why not? _____

_____

_____

What did you **do** when you got angry? Did you hurt anyone because of your anger?

_____

_____

What happened next? Did the problem get better or worse? _____

_____

_____

What did you **want** to happen? _____

_____

Were you successful in getting what you wanted? _____

What else could you have done to try to solve your problem that would not have involved hurting anyone?

_____

Name _____ Date _____

Solving Problems Without Hurting Anyone

Think of three things that have made you angry in the past. Identify the problem, what you **wanted** to happen, and what you could have done to solve the problem **without hurting anyone.**

1. Problem: _____

_____

_____

   I wanted: _____

_____

   I could have: _____

_____

2. Problem: _____

_____

   I wanted: _____

_____

   I could have: _____

_____

3. Problem: _____

_____

   I wanted: _____

_____

   I could have: _____

_____

Name _____ Date _____

Ways Of Dealing with Anger

There are many things you *could* do when you get angry. Here are some things some people have done.

1. Pounded their fists on their desks.
2. Yelled and screamed at everybody around them so that others would know they were angry.
3. Walked away and tried to forget they were angry.
4. Counted to 10 before doing anything.
5. Hurt the people who made them angry.
6. Talked to the people who made them angry and explained why they were angry.
7. Talked to their parents or teachers about their problems and why they were angry.
8. Did something fun so they would be happy instead of angry.
9. Asked themselves if they really had a good reason to be angry.
10. Tried to understand the reasons why the people who angered them did so.

List some other things that you have seen people do when they were angry.

11. _____

12. _____

13. _____

14. _____

15. _____

Which of these things might be most helpful for you to do when you are angry?

_____

_____

_____

Why? _____

_____

_____

Name _____ Date _____

Put all of the things you could do when you are angry (from the list on the previous page) in order from most helpful (1) to least helpful (15).

1. _____

2. _____

3. _____

4. _____

5. _____

6. _____

7. _____

8. _____

9. _____

10. _____

11. _____

12. _____

13. _____

14. _____

15. _____

Making a Plan For The Future

Make a plan for what you will do about a problem that made you angry. (For example, write an apology to someone you hurt.)

_____

_____

_____

_____

STRESS MANAGEMENT

Tips for the Teacher

Stress is a physical and psychological condition experienced whenever demands are placed on an individual to adapt or change. The challenge for students is to make sure that their ability to cope at least matches their level of stress. When coping skills are inadequate (creating a bad stress or **distress**), students can be expected to suffer in a number of ways including productivity and general effectiveness in the classroom. Teachers are important resources for students who need assistance in dealing with the stress in their lives.

Suggestions for Helping Students Manage Stress:

Know symptoms. The negative effects of stress are diverse in nature and fall into four general categories:

* *Physical:* In the short run, individuals experience various signs of physiological arousal (e.g., sweaty palms, trembling hands, increased respiration). As stress continues over a long period of time, poor physical health may occur in such forms as increased susceptibility to illness, headaches, chronic fatigue, and lowered energy.

* *Affective:* Anxiety is the hallmark symptom of stress, but other affective symptoms may include anger, depression, irritability, and joylessness.

* *Cognitive:* Disruptions in normal cognitive functioning include poor judgment, forgetfulness, inability to concentrate, excessive worrying, lack of attention to details, and negative thinking.

* *Behavioral:* Behavior changes may include restlessness, poor school performance, poor communication with others (including isolation, withdrawal, and non-involvement), escape and avoidance tactics, excessive accidents, and behavioral excesses (such as overeating).

Knowing these symptoms can help teachers recognize stress in their students. Students should be taught to recognize the symptoms in themselves and to take appropriate actions to deal with the stress.

Know sources. Common sources of stress (**stressors**) for students include:

* *Frustration:* Students get frustrated when they are unable to achieve desired goals. These students may be having difficulty coping with delays, lack of resources (e.g., lack of some skill), losses (e.g., loss of friendship), failures, or loneliness.

45

* *Conflict:* Students face a variety of conflicts in which they must choose between incompatible goals. They may want to study for an important exam, but they also want to go to a movie with friends. They must choose one goal over the other.

* *Pressure:* External pressure (e.g., from parents and peers) and internal pressure (i.e., pressure put on oneself) involve demands or challenges to perform in certain ways.

* *Overload:* Sometimes students are overwhelmed by the feeling they have too much to do and too little time in which to do it.

* *Life events and daily hassles:* Major life events such as a death or divorce in the family are major sources of stress for some students, but even more significant are daily hassles—the petty, everyday annoyances that irritate people. These hassles vary across age groups and individuals, but common ones are losing things, worrying about one's physical appearance, and taking tests.

By being aware of these various origins of stress, teachers can help students identify the nature of their difficulties and thus better pinpoint possible coping strategies.

Know coping strategies. Again, the key is to control stress through effective coping. A number of strategies are available:

* *Planned action-taking:* This strategy involves directly attacking the problem. If it is determined, for example, that one's stress is due in large part to time management problems, an obvious and appropriate coping strategy is to improve one's time management skills. In general, students who take direct action might seek help, work to develop needed skills, lower demands, or find ways to lessen the occurrence or intensity of daily hassles.

* *Cognitive control:* This strategy involves changing one's perceptions and viewing otherwise distressing situations in more positive, optimistic ways. It might mean lowering one's perfectionism, having realistic expectations, not seeing everything in highly threatening and catastrophic terms, and not overgeneralizing from one negative situation (e.g., students sometimes conclude that they will never suc- ceed in life when they do poorly on one exam in one subject). Monitoring one's self- talk and making it more positive and hopeful is the challenge.

* *Social support:* Students cope better when they have at least one person they can count on for support during difficult times, whether that person is a parent, another family member, a friend, or perhaps even a teacher.

* *Physical condition:* A good diet, adequate sleep, and proper exercise are all critical in dealing with stress.

* *Hardiness:* People seem to manage stress better when they possess a personality style referred to as hardiness. A "hardy" student is one who approaches stressful situations by seeing them as challenges, by perceiving control over them, and by being committed to the activities of their lives.

* *Predictability:* Knowing what to anticipate about an event makes it easier to handle. The greater the knowledge and the less the uncertainty in a difficult situation, the better.

* *Uplifts:* If a person is plagued with a number of negative situations in life, one antidote is to develop uplifts or positive experiences that can help offset the negative ones.

* *Relaxation:* It is important that students find ways to relax on a regular basis in order to counteract the physiological effects of stress.

* *Personal anchors:* Personal anchors give life meaning and purpose. They might include certain beliefs (such as religious beliefs), daily routines, special events or activities, favorite places, or meaningful objects. In any case, they are relatively stable and unchanging through time. They give an individual some stability in the midst of difficulties.

Teachers' knowledge of these various coping techniques can be of great benefit when students need advice and guidance regarding stress management.

Suggestions for Individual or Group Activities:

* Discuss with the class the various symptoms of stress so that students will be in a better position to identify and label stress when they are experiencing it and will, therefore, be better able to deal with it.

* As a class activity, discuss some stressful situations and possible solutions. Address issues like loss of friendship, separating parents, adjustments to new situations (e.g., moving to a new town or school), or sibling conflicts. Discuss possible consequences of not coping.

* Talk with the class about the meaning of optimism and pessimism. Point out that someone's ability to cope with a stressful situation could be affected by his tendency to be optimistic or pessimistic. Discuss optimistic and pessimistic feelings about such things as going to the dentist, taking a test, buying a gift for a friend, or moving.

* Have students share demonstrations of hobbies or special interests with the class. Schedule the demonstrations throughout the school year. Such an activity should be useful to those students who lack outlets for finding relaxation and a sense of purposefulness in their lives.

* Post in the classroom a list of "Helpful Hints for Dealing with Stress" (see an example of such a list on page 55). Discuss the hints with students. Get their reactions and help them interpret the suggestions.

* Stress **can** be a very serious problem. If a student is experiencing severe stress-related symptoms, professional counseling may be necessary.

Bibliography

Goleman, D. (1995). *Emotional intelligence.* New York: Bantam.

Greenberg, J. S. (1996). *Comprehensive stress management* (5th ed.). Madison, WI: Brown & Benchmark.

Prokop, C. K. (1991). Stress and illness. In V. J. Derlega, B. A. Winstead, & W. H. Jones (Eds.), *Personality: Contemporary theory and research* (pp. 481–508). Chicago: Nelson-Hall.

Rice, P. L. (1987). *Stress and health: Principles and practice for coping and wellness.* Monterey, CA: Brooks/Cole.

Schafer, W. (1987). *Stress management for wellness.* New York: Holt, Rinehart and Winston.

Scheier, M. F., & Carver, C. S. (1993). On the power of positive thinking: The benefits of being optimistic. *Current Directions in Psychological Science, 2,* 26–30.

Seligman, M. E. P. (1990). *Learned optimism.* New York: Knopf.

Name _____ Date _____

Measuring Your Coping Ability

People experience stress when there are demands placed upon them. Stress can be handled effectively if a person has adequate coping skills. How well are you able to manage the stress in your life? Answering the following items may help you figure out how good a coper you are and how much improvement you may still need to make.

Circle the number and word or phrase that make each statement true for you.

1. I enjoy exercise.

0	1	2	3
never	rarely	often	very often

2. I eat a balanced diet.

0	1	2	3
never	rarely	often	very often

3. I feel like things will turn out for the best.

0	1	2	3
never	rarely	often	very often

4. I manage my time well.

0	1	2	3
never	rarely	often	very often

5. I get enough sleep.

0	1	2	3
never	rarely	often	very often

6. I talk to my friends or my family when I am troubled about something.

0	1	2	3
never	rarely	often	very often

7. I like to laugh.

0	1	2	3
never	rarely	often	very often

Name _____ Date _____

8. I find ways to relax and do fun things.

0	1	2	3
never	rarely	often	very often

9. I view difficult situations as challenges to overcome.

0	1	2	3
never	rarely	often	very often

10. I believe I can control what happens to me in life.

0	1	2	3
never	rarely	often	very often

Add up the numbers you circled. The total is your **Coping Ability Score.**

My score is: _____

0–10 points: Coping with stress may be a problem for you. Talk to your teacher about things you can do.

11–20 points: You're doing some good things, but you need to improve your coping ability even more. Talk to your teacher for advice on what you can do.

21–30 points: You appear to be doing many of the things that good copers do. Your chances of experiencing negative effects of stress are reduced considerably because of your good coping ability.

Do you agree with your **Coping Ability Score**? _____ Why? _____

_____

_____

Would your teachers agree with you about your score? _____ Why? _____

_____

_____

Would your parents agree with you about your score? _____ Why? _____

_____

_____

Name _____ Date _____

Common Stressful Situations

List the three most common stressful situations that you face.

1._____

2._____

3._____

Circle the numbers of the most typical reactions you have when you are experiencing a lot of stress in your life and are not coping well.

1. trembling hands	10. worrying	18. withdrawal from others
2. headaches	11. forgetfulness	19. criticism of others
3. illness	12. negative thinking	20. difficulty communicating
4. fatigue	13. poor judgment	with others
5. anxiety	14. self-criticism	21. little energy
6. anger	15. restlessness	22. accidents
7. depression	16. poor school performance	23. lack of attention to details
8. irritability	17. overeating	24. crying
9. lack of concentration		25. arguments with others

What other reactions do you commonly have? _____

_____

The statements below and on the next page reflect some good ways people can deal with stress. Circle the numbers of the ways you usually cope with stressful situations.

1. Talk to family and friends about my problem.
2. Find ways to relax and have fun even when faced with difficult situations.
3. Find ways to solve my problem and then develop a plan for doing so.
4. Make sure I'm eating well, exercising, and getting enough sleep.
5. Ask for help.
6. Go over the situation in my mind and try to understand it.
7. View the stressful situation as an interesting challenge to overcome.
8. Try to learn as much as I can about my problem so I can deal with it better.
9. When possible, try to eliminate some of the demands placed on me.
10. Try to find something positive and good about my difficult situation.

Name _____ Date _____

11. Realize that things could be a lot worse than they are.

12. Remain hopeful and optimistic that things will get better.

13. Try not to expect things to be perfect all the time.

14. Try to be realistic about what to expect.

15. Believe that I can control my problems and my stress.

Which of the 15 coping strategies do you think would be the most helpful or effective in dealing with your most common stressful situations?

1. _____

2. _____

3. _____

Why do you feel that these would be the most helpful?

_____

_____

_____

Which of the 15 coping strategies do you think would be the least helpful or effective in dealing with your most common stressful situations?

1. _____

2. _____

3. _____

Why do you feel that these would be the least helpful?

_____

_____

_____

Name _____ Date _____

A Stressful Situation

Describe a situation that is stressful for you right now. _____

_____

_____

Describe how the situation has been affecting your feelings, thoughts, actions, and physical health.

1. My feelings: _____

_____

2. My thoughts: _____

_____

3. My actions: _____

_____

4. My physical health: _____

_____

How have you been coping with the situation up to this point? _____

_____

_____

Have your coping strategies been working for you and making the situation better? Why or why not?

_____

_____

What do you **want** to happen?_____

_____

_____

Name _____ Date _____

List three new strategies you might use in coping with the situation. (Discuss this matter with your teacher if you need help.)

1. _____

2. _____

3. _____

Which of the above strategies do you think would be the most helpful in dealing with the stressful situation?

_____

Why? _____

_____

_____

Develop a plan for what you will do now in dealing with this situation. Be specific.

_____

_____

_____

_____

_____

_____

_____

_____

_____

If your plan proves to be unsuccessful,
discuss the situation with your teacher.

HELPFUL HINTS FOR DEALING WITH STRESS

1. Be responsible for managing your own stress.

2. Know the symptoms of stress. Know when you are experiencing more stress than you are able to handle.

3. Be able to identify the reasons for your stress.

4. If necessary, make a plan and take action:
   * Find ways to reduce the stress in your life.
   * Find ways to cope better with the stress in your life.

5. Balance the stress in your life:
   * A little stress is good.
   * Too much stress is bad.

6. Be patient. Don't try to solve all of your stress problems at once.

7. Don't rely on a single stress management strategy.

8. Realize that stress management is an ongoing, never-ending process.

9. Be optimistic.

10. Take charge. Make your life better.

WORKING EFFECTIVELY WITH OTHERS

Tips for the Teacher

Whether in the classroom, on the job, or in life in general, people need certain *interpersonal skills* in order to optimize their success. They need to be able to resolve conflicts, communicate effectively, work effectively in groups, cooperate, share, support others' goals, empathize with others, assertively (nonhurtfully) express their rights and views, accept constructive criticism, respect others, tolerate differences between themselves and others, negotiate, compromise, actively listen, treat each other fairly, apologize when appropriate, show patience, be flexible when needed, be honest and trustworthy, and avoid behaviors that tend to alienate and antagonize others.

Suggestions for Helping Students Work Effectively With Others:

Establish common goals and conditions of interdependence. Cooperation can be fostered through multiple opportunities for students to share a common interest or goal in which each person's unique contributions are required to achieve that goal.

Teach students conflict resolution skills. Emphasize the importance of: 1) identifying the problem; 2) becoming aware of the possible causes of the problem, including one's beliefs (e.g., "I must have everything my way") and one's feelings (e.g., jealousy); 3) searching for solutions; 4) choosing and implementing the best solution—one that achieves a "win-win" outcome for all parties; 5) evaluating the effectiveness of the solution; and 6) trying a new solution if the first one proves ineffective.

Teach communication skills. Use modeling, coaching, behavioral rehearsal (role-playing), feedback, and reinforcement to teach students specific communication skills such as initiating conversations, asserting themselves, making eye contact, smiling, sharing information about themselves, taking turns in conversation (and not dominating the conversation), showing interest in others by asking questions, not interrupting, responding to what was just said, disagreeing in a nonthreatening manner (not insulting), complimenting, joining, inviting, not blaming, not arguing with everything someone says, asking for help when needed, offering help and suggestions, and showing more interest in the other person than oneself.

Establish a positive classroom environment. Teachers can contribute much to their students' effective working relationships by displaying self-confidence and establishing relationships with students characterized by dignity, respect, honesty, fairness, attention and recognition, caring, high expectations, and consistency.

Be alert to relationship obstacles. Students characterized by low self-esteem, disparate backgrounds and personalities, or various prejudices will have some difficulty in their relationships. Relationships are hindered as well when students are excessively hostile and suspicious, overly dependent on others, or aloof. Such matters need to be addressed by teachers.

Suggestions for Individual or Group Activities:

* Make expectations clear regarding what is proper or improper behavior when relating to others. This could be done, for example, through class discussions, verbal reminders, and written statements (student handbook, classroom poster).

* Look for examples of students behaving in appropriate ways throughout the day. Award certificates for such behaviors as helping or encouraging each other.

* Challenge the students as a class to work together toward a common goal. For example, require "good behavior" from every student during a given day in order for the entire class to gain a privilege like extra computer time, or require good class behavior for an extended time in order to earn a larger privilege like watching a movie.

* Role-play conflict resolution strategies with students. Put various hypothetical conflict scenarios on slips of paper and distribute them to groups of students for discussion and solution. As each group presents its conflict and solution, the rest of the class should provide feedback and possible alternative solutions. Prior to the discussion, help students plan their analysis by identifying with them the conflict resolution steps noted on the previous page.

* For students to work well together, they need to read each other's emotions, which are often communicated nonverbally. Have students play charades, acting out and reading various emotional states such as sadness, anger, and shyness. This exercise encourages students' ability to see things from another's perspective (role-taking). From that, students hopefully will be better able to empathize, whereby they actually share another's feelings.

* Develop a "good deed" coupon system in which students can give coupons to others in the class. A coupon given by one student to another amounts to an offer to do a good deed for that student (e.g., the coupon might say "I volunteer to help you after school with your math assignment."). The exercise should encourage role-taking and empathy skills and help establish a positive classroom environment conducive to good interpersonal relations.

Bibliography

Arbetter, S. R. (1991, September). Resolving conflicts step by step. *Current Health 2*, pp. 14–15.

Bierman, K. L., & Furman, W. (1984). The effects of social skills training and peer involvement on the social adjustment of preadolescents. *Child Development, 55*, 151–162.

Branden, N. (1994). *The six pillars of self-esteem.* New York: Bantam.

Bukatko, D., & Daehler, M. W. (1992). *Child development: A topical approach.* Boston: Houghton Mifflin.

Dawis, R. V., & Fruehling, R. T. (1996). *Psychology: Realizing human potential* (8th ed.). St. Paul, MN: Paradigm.

Goleman, D. (1995). *Emotional intelligence.* New York: Bantam.

Name _____ Date _____

Working with Others

Success in the classroom and life in general requires that you be able to work effectively with others. How well are you able to do this? The list below describes behaviors or characteristics that a person might display when relating to others. Put a plus (+) in front of those items that you think are good and helpful when working with others and a minus (-) in front of those you think are bad and would therefore cause problems.

_____ A person takes turns talking during conversations.

_____ A person does most of the talking during conversations.

_____ A person listens while others are talking.

_____ A person interrupts others while they are talking.

_____ A person compromises when needed.

_____ A person makes sure he always gets his own way.

_____ A person is considerate of others.

_____ A person is respectful of others' feelings.

_____ A person is willing to discuss others' ideas.

_____ A person is selfish.

_____ A person is willing to share.

_____ A person is willing to solve problems peacefully and fairly.

_____ A person blames others when things go wrong.

_____ A person is reliable.

_____ A person is impatient with others.

_____ A person asks others what they think.

_____ A person refuses to ask for help when it is needed.

_____ A person shows no concern for others.

_____ A person quits when he doesn't get his way.

_____ A person invites others to join his group.

_____ A person gets mad easily.

_____ A person gets his feelings hurt easily.

_____ A person gives others sincere compliments.

_____ A person gives others credit for doing a good job.

_____ A person keeps his thoughts and feelings to himself.

_____ A person stands up for his rights.

_____ A person reacts to criticism by trying to improve.

_____ A person refuses to apologize for a mistake.

_____ A person lies to others.

Name _____ Date _____

_____ A person becomes jealous of others' successes.

_____ A person encourages others to do their best.

_____ A person argues with everyone.

_____ A person hurts people when he doesn't get his way.

_____ A person is accepting of others even when they are different from him.

_____ A person goofs off and lets everyone else do all the work.

_____ A person pitches in and does his share of the work.

_____ A person is flexible when needed.

_____ A person does not look at others when they are talking.

_____ A person helps others in need.

_____ A person tries to show off and impress others.

Think of someone you like to work with. What are three behaviors or characteristics you see when *that person* works with others? In other words, *why* do you like to work with this person?

1._____

2._____

3._____

From the list on the previous page and above, pick the three items that **best** describe you when you work with others in a good way.

1._____

2._____

3._____

Do you think most people find you easy to work with? _____ yes _____ no (check one)

Why or why not?

_____

_____

_____

Name _____ Date _____

List three good things that happen when you are able to work well with others.

1. _____

2. _____

3. _____

List three bad things that happen when you are not able to work well with others.

1. _____

2. _____

3. _____

Again, from the earlier list, pick three items that **best** describe behaviors you need to improve when working with others.

1. _____

2. _____

3. _____

With those three items in mind, set some specific goals you would like to achieve. What exactly would you like to accomplish?

1. _____

2. _____

3. _____

Now make a plan for what you will do in the future to achieve your goals. Be specific. What are the exact steps you will have to take to be able to work with others in better ways?

_____

_____

_____

_____